# The Blueprint for UI/UX Design

# Creating Digital Products People Love

Taylor Royce

# DEDICATION

To all the innovative thinkers and enthusiastic designers who toil nonstop to produce valuable and captivating user experiences.

To my family and friends, who have consistently inspired me with their steadfast support and encouragement.

To the innumerable users whose opinions and suggestions motivate us to keep developing and innovating.

And to the next generation of designers: may you always act with empathy and honesty as you explore the limits of creativity and technology.

You should read this book.

# CONTENTS

# ACKNOWLEDGMENTS

The inspiration, mentorship, and assistance of numerous people were essential to the completion of this work.

I want to start by sincerely thanking my family for everything. I have gotten my strength and inspiration to follow my passions from your constant support and encouragement.

I appreciate all of your advice, friendship, and support, friends and colleagues in the design and technology sectors. We are always inspired by your commitment to quality and creativity.

A particular thanks goes out to all of the users who have shared their experiences, offered feedback, and taken part in usability tests. The field of UI/UX design has advanced thanks to your critical feedback that shaped the content of this book.

As their expertise and insight have aided me throughout my career, I am also appreciative of my mentors and teachers. As a designer and a professional, your lessons have been invaluable to my development.

Thank you for your hard work and dedication in making this book a reality, editors, and reviewers of the publishing team. This book is of the greatest caliber thanks to your skill and attention to detail.

I'd like to end by thanking each and every one of you for reading this book and showing interest in UI/UX design. In addition to being a useful tool, I hope this book will motivate you to design experiences that are both creative and user-focused.

I am truly grateful,

# DISCLAIMER

This book's content aims to provide direction and insights based on the most recent knowledge and methods in the UI/UX design industry. Although every attempt has been taken to guarantee the correctness and applicability of the data offered, it is crucial to remember that technology and design concepts are always changing.

The material provided is not guaranteed to be free from mistakes or omissions, and the author and publisher disclaims all liability for any repercussions that may result from using or misinterpreting the information. It is recommended that readers exercise critical thinking and refer to supplementary materials as needed.

You understand and agree that the content in this book is being sold exclusively for informational and educational reasons by purchasing it. Any negative repercussions or results arising from the implementation of the content are not the responsibility of the author or publisher.

We appreciate your input and invite you to provide

thoughtful, insightful commentary on your experiences. For a resolution, please contact the author or publisher directly if you have any questions or reservations with the content.

I appreciate your help and understanding.

# CHAPTER 1

## UI/UX Design Overview

## 1.1 The User Experience's Evolution

Since its conception, user experience (UX) design has experienced a substantial evolution. At first, usability making sure that consumers could interact with things in an efficient manner was the main focus of user experience (UX). But as technology advanced, so did user expectations and interface complexity.

### Early Beginnings

- The History of Human-Computer Interaction (HCI) The field of human-computer interaction serves as the basis for UX design. The goal of early research was to improve computer usability and accessibility for non-experts.
- **Psychology of cognition:** Understanding how people perceive, remember, and interact with

1

interfaces was made possible in large part by discoveries made in the field of cognitive psychology.

## The Digital Revolution

- The Rise of Personal Computing throughout the Digital Revolution The 1980s saw the introduction of personal computers, which increased the demand for user-friendly interfaces. User-friendly design started to become a top priority for companies like Apple and Microsoft.
- **The Age of the Internet:** With the advent of the internet in the 1990s, new design techniques were required to manage online interactions and navigation.

## Contemporary UX Design

- **Mobile Revolution:** The advent of smartphones brought about a revolution in UX design by placing a strong emphasis on touch interfaces and responsive design.
- **Emergence of UX Professionals:** Specialized education and training programs helped to codify the

work of UX designers.

- **Comprehensive User Experience:** These days, user experience (UX) includes not only usability but also overall satisfaction, emotional effect, and aesthetics.

## 1.2 The Benefits of Good UI/UX for Business

Investing in UI/UX design effectively has significant business ramifications in addition to producing visually appealing interfaces.

### Increasing Customer Satisfaction

- **Enhanced Usability:** A well-thought-out interface facilitates users in reaching their objectives, which raises satisfaction.
- **Nice Emotional Effect:** Positive emotional reactions are elicited by aesthetically beautiful and intuitive designs, which promote client loyalty.

### Increasing Conversions and Sales

- **Streamlined Purchase Process:** User-friendly interfaces make the purchasing process less complicated, which boosts conversion rates.

- **Increased Engagement:** Interactive designs entice users to stay on the platform longer, which increases the chance that they will make a purchase.

## Cutting Expenses

- **Fewer Support Requests:** Because intuitive design requires less customer support, operational expenses are decreased.
- **Decreased Development Time:** Well-considered and concise UI/UX lessens the need for in-depth redesigns and modifications, which saves time and money.

## Competitive Advantage

- **Brand Differentiation:** A company's ability to differentiate itself from the competition through exceptional UI/UX can become a crucial differentiator in the market.
- **Customer Retention:** Because happy customers are more likely to come back, positive user experiences increase customer retention rates.

# 1.3 User-Centered Design's Fundamentals

A framework known as user-centered design (UCD) centers the design process on the user, guaranteeing that their requirements, preferences, and constraints are taken into account at every turn.

## Comprehending User Needs

- **User Research:** Surveys, interviews, and usability tests are carried out to obtain information about user preferences and behavior.
- **Personas:** Developing thorough user personas to inform design choices.

## Iterative Design Process

- The Iterative Design Process involves the development of both high-fidelity and low-fidelity prototypes in order to investigate various design options.
- **User Testing:** Testing prototypes frequently with actual users in order to get their input and improve the design.

## Accessibility

- **Inclusive Design:** Making sure the product complies with best practices and accessibility requirements so that users with impairments may use it.
- **Responsive Design:** Designing user interfaces that adapt to different screen sizes and devices with ease.

## Usability

- **Simplicity:** To reduce user effort, keep the design straightforward and uncomplicated.
- **Consistency:** Preserving uniformity in design components to establish a dependable user experience.

## Aesthetics

- **Visual Appeal:** Producing eye-catching designs that complement the identity of the company.
- **Emotional Design:** Taking into account how design elements may affect users' emotions in order to produce a satisfying user experience.

# 1.4 Distinguishing Between User Experience and User Interface

Despite their frequent interchangeability, UI and UX refer to different areas of design.

## User Interface (UI)

**Definition:** The graphical design of an application, comprising icons, buttons, and other visual components, is referred to as the UI.

## Priorities:

- **Design:** Developing the appearance and texture of the product.
- **Interaction Design:** Specifying how users engage with elements of the interface.
- **Typography and Colors:** Choosing suitable typefaces and color schemes to improve readability and visual appeal.

## User Experience (UX)

**Definition:** UX includes a user's feelings, perceptions, and level of satisfaction with a product as a whole.

**Main Areas of Interest:**

- **User Research:** Comprehending user requirements and actions.
- **Information Architecture:** Organizing information so that it is simple to access and comprehend.
- **Usability Testing:** Constantly testing and refining the product in response to customer input.

**How UI and UX Are Related**

- **Complementary Roles:** Together, UI and UX produce a seamless and entertaining user experience. Whereas UI concentrates on the interactive and visual elements, UX makes sure the product fulfills user requirements and offers a satisfying user experience.
- **Collaborative Process:** To provide the best outcomes, effective design teams closely collaborate with designers from each discipline, integrating UI and UX processes.

It is critical for everyone involved in the design process to comprehend the history of user experience, the financial benefits of successful UI/UX, the fundamentals of user-centered design, and the distinctions between UI and UX. Through putting the user first at every turn and understanding the many functions of UI and UX, companies can design products that are not just useful and effective but also enjoyable to use.

# CHAPTER 2

## 2.1 Approaches for User Research

One of the most important aspects of UI/UX design is user understanding. A variety of user research approaches can be used by designers to get insight into the demands, behaviors, and pain areas of their users.

### Interviews with Users

- **Definition:** Direct talks with users are conducted during user interviews in order to learn about their experiences, preferences, and difficulties.

### Workflow:

- **Preparation:** Create a series of open-ended inquiries covering the main topics of interest.
- **Conducting Interviews:** Talk to people in a relaxed

environment and encourage them to openly express their opinions.

- **Analysis:** Examine and group the answers to find recurring themes and ideas.

## Features:

- Offers comprehensive qualitative data.
- Makes it possible to interpret user reactions in real time.
- Discovers surprising revelations.

## Questionnaires and Surveys

- **Definition:** Questionnaires and surveys are instruments for gathering numerical data from a sizable user population.

## Workflow:

- **Creating the Survey:** Use a combination of multiple-choice, rating scale, and open-ended questions to craft precise and succinct questions.
- **Distribution:** Make the survey available via a variety of platforms, including social media, email,

and the product itself.

- **Analysis:** Examine replies using statistical techniques to spot patterns.

## Features:

- Quickly compiles information from a big audience.
- Offers quantitative information suitable for statistical analysis.
- Recognizes more general user patterns and tendencies.

## Testing for Usability

- **Definition:** To find usability problems with a product, usability testers watch people interact with it.

## Process:

- **Planning:** Establish test goals, make test plans, and find representative users.
- **Conducting Tests:** Lead user-perform task sessions while observers record notes.
- **Analysis:** Examine notes and recordings to find

usability problems and potential areas for development.

## Features:

- Offers firsthand perceptions about user interactions.
- Defines certain pain areas and usability concerns.
- Enables testing and improvement through iterations.

## Comparative Evaluation

- **Definition:** In A/B testing, the performance of two variants of a design is compared.

## Process:

- **Designing Variants:** Produce two renditions of the design, with one major component (such as button color or layout) different.
- **Implementation:** Assign users at random to every version while gathering performance information.
- **Analysis:** Compare the outcomes to ascertain which variant more successfully accomplishes the intended result.

## Features:

- Offers empirical proof of the efficacy of the design.
- Assists in maximizing particular design components.
- Encourages decision-making based on data.

## Analytical

- **Definition:** Analytics is the study of behavior and performance through the use of data gathered from user interactions.

## Process:

- **Setup:** Utilize analytics software to monitor user activities, including page views, clicks, and conversions.
- **Data Collection:** As consumers engage with the product, data is continuously gathered.
- **Analysis:** Look for patterns, user flows, and drop-off points using analytics dashboards.

## Features:

- Delivers data continuously and in real time.
- Provides broad insights into user activity.

- Encourages ongoing observation and development.

## 2.2 Creating Personas for Users

User personas are fictitious depictions of target users that are developed using actual data and research-derived insights.

### User Personas' Importance

- **Empathy:** Assists designers in comprehending and feeling the requirements and objectives of various user segments.
- **Alignment:** Guarantees that everyone in the team is aware of who the target audience is.
- **Focus**: Maintains the user in the center of design decisions.

### The User Persona Creation Process

- **Data Collection:** Compile information from user research, both quantitative and qualitative.
- **Segmentation:** Determine shared traits and divide users into several groups.
- **Persona Development:** Construct thorough

personas that include:

- **Demographics**: Gender, age, profession, level of education, etc.
- **Behaviors:** Patterns of usage, inclinations, problems, etc.
- **Objectives:** Both primary and secondary product-related objectives.
- **Quotes:** To give the persona to life, representative quotes from actual users.
- **Validation:** Examine and improve personas in consultation with stakeholders and extra user input.

## Advantages of Using User Personas:

- **Better Design:** Guarantees that designs are customized to match the unique requirements of intended users.
- **Enhanced Communication:** Promotes improved team alignment and communication.
- **Targeted Marketing:** By comprehending user groups, it assists in developing more successful marketing methods.

## 2.3 Making Maps of User Journeys

User journey maps show the steps a user takes to use a product to accomplish a particular objective.

**The elements that comprise a user journey map are as follows:**

- **Stages:** Important stages that the user experiences (e.g., discovery, consideration, purchase, post-buy).
- **Touchpoints:** User interactions with the product at every level.
- **Actions:** Particular steps the user takes at every point of contact.
- **Emotions:** The user's emotional reactions and pain areas.
- **Opportunities:** Improvement opportunities noted at every level.

**User Journey Map Creation Process**

- **Define Objectives:** Clearly state the purpose and parameters of the journey map.
- **Research**: Compile information from surveys, analytics, and user interviews.

- **Mapping:** Draw out the user experience visually, emphasizing important emotions and touchpoints.
- **Analysis:** Determine areas of concern and chances to improve the user experience.
- **Validation:** Discuss the journey map with relevant parties and make revisions in response to comments.

## Advantages of User Journey Maps:

- **Holistic View:** Offers a thorough comprehension of the user experience at various phases.
- **Identification of Pain Points:** Points out trouble spots for users so that design can be improved.
- **Enhanced Collaboration**: Promotes improved stakeholder and team communication and alignment.

## 2.4 Showing Users Empathy

Understanding consumers' viewpoints, feelings, and wants via empathy is essential for producing more efficient and human-centered design solutions.

## The Value of Empathy in Design

- **User-Centric Solutions:** Guarantees that designs

take into account the requirements and difficulties of actual users.

- **Emotional Connection:** Produces goods that emotionally connect with customers in order to build brand loyalty.
- **Problem-Solving:** Aids designers in foreseeing and more skillfully resolving user issues.

**Methods for Developing Empathy with Users:**
- **User Shadowing:** Watching users in their element to gain insight into their mindset and actions.
- **Empathy Maps:** Visual aids that assist in capturing users' thoughts, feelings, words, and actions in order to present a comprehensive picture of their experience.
- **Role-Playing:** Imagining oneself in the user's position in order to see the product through their eyes.

**Advantages of User Empathy:**
- **Improved User Satisfaction:** Produces designs that surpass users' expectations and fulfill their needs.
- **Innovative Solutions:** Promotes original thinking in

solving problems by closely analyzing user problems.

- **Stronger User Relationships:** Fosters rapport and trust with users, which encourages steadfast commitment.

Effective and user-centered design requires a thorough understanding of the user through a variety of research approaches, the creation of user personas, user journey maps, and an ability to empathize with people. Designers may create products that meet functional requirements and provide great user delight by putting user needs and experiences first.

# CHAPTER 3

## Innovation and Design Thinking

## 3.1 The Methodology of Design Thinking

A user-centered method of problem-solving that encourages creativity is called design thinking. It places a strong emphasis on comprehending users, questioning presumptions, redefining issues, and coming up with creative prototype and testing solutions. There are five main steps to this highly collaborative iterative approach.

### Design Thinking Process Stages

### 1. Empathize

- **Objective**: Recognize the needs, goals, and difficulties of the user.
- **Processes:**
  - User interviews
  - Observations

    ○  Surveys

**Results:** Acquire in-depth knowledge about user experiences and problem spots.

## 2. Define

- **Objective:** Clearly state the issue that has to be resolved.
- **Applications:**
  - ○ Forming User Personas
  - ○ Formulating Issue Statements

**Result:** A targeted issue statement that directs the brainstorming session.

## 3. Ideate

- **Objective:** Come up with a variety of concepts and solutions.
- **Methods:**
  - ○ Brainstorming
  - ○ Mind Mapping
  - ○ Sketching

**Outcome:** A broad range of viable answers.

## 4. Prototype

- **Objective:** Construct clear, concrete models of your concepts.
- **Actions:**
  - Structures: Wireframes,
  - Mockups
  - Concrete Models

**Result**: Prototypes of low fidelity that are testable and scalable.

## 5. Test

- **Goal:** Verify your solutions with actual customers.
- **Methods:**
  - Usability Testing
  - User Feedback Sessions

**Outcome:** Refined solutions based on user feedback, leading to additional iterations.

## 3.2 Methods of Ideation

In the design thinking process, ideation is a crucial stage where original solutions to the stated problem are produced. Divergent thinking is needed to consider a variety of options.

# Crucial Idea Generators

## 1. Brainstorming

- **Objective:** Promote original thought and produce a large number of ideas.
- **Applications:**
  - Group Meetings
  - The No Criticism Rule
  - Quantity Over Quality

**Outcome:** A broad selection of unique ideas.

## 2. Mind Mapping

- **Objective:** Examine connections and arrange ideas visually.
- **Applications:**
  - Main Idea
  - Branching Concepts
  - Sub-branches

**Result:** An ordered illustration of concepts and their connections.

## 3. SCAMPER

- **Objective:** Question and change pre existing concepts to innovate.
- **Actions:**
  - One can substitute, combine, adapt, modify, or put to another use.
  - Remove
  - Turn Around

**Result:** Fresh insights and creative fixes.

## 4. Sketching

- **Objective**: Quickly sketch up notions and ideas.
- The following are the **Methods:**
  - Quick sketches,
  - storyboards,
  - diagrams

**Result:** Easily communicated and iterated upon visual representations.

## 5. Six Thinking Hats

- **Objective:** Consider an issue from several angles.
- **Actions:**
  a. **Red Hat:** Emotions and Feelings
  b. **White Hat:** Facts and Information

c. **Yellow Hat:** Optimism and Benefits

d. **Black Hat:** Caution and Critical Thinking

e. **Green Hat:** Innovation and Substitutes

f. **Blue Hat:** Process Control

**Result:** A comprehensive analysis of the issue and possible fixes.

## 3.3 Iteration and Prototyping

Iteration and prototyping are crucial for bringing concepts to life and improving them in response to user input. This procedure aids in finding errors, evaluating features, and enhancing the design.

## Making prototypes

## 1. Low-Fidelity Prototypes

- **Objective:** Quickly sketch out conceptual frameworks.
- **Approaches:**
  - Paper Prototypes
  - Sketches
  - Wireframe Development

**Result:** Preliminary ideas that are easily adaptable.

## 2. High-Fidelity Prototypes

- **Goal:** Create intricate and interactive models.
- **Actions:**
  - Electronic prototypes
  - Clickable Working Models
  - Models of Function

**Result:** Prototypes that are realistic and nearly identical to the finished product.

## Repetition

## 1. User Testing

- **Goal:** Test prototypes on actual users.
- **Actions:**
  - User feedback sessions
  - Usability tests

**Result:** Understanding of user behavior and opportunities for enhancement.

## 2. Feedback Integration

- **Goal:** Integrate user input into the design process.

- **Actions:**
  - ○ Examining Input
  - ○ Setting Priorities for Modifications
  - ○ Making Prototypes Better

**Result:** Improved prototypes that are more user-friendly.

## 3. Continuous Improvement

- **Goal:** Improve the design by going through several iterations.
- Applications:
  - ○ Iterative Testing
  - ○ Gradual Improvements

**Result:** A refined and user-tested design.

## 3.4 Innovation through Design

Designing for innovation entails coming up with ground-breaking as well as practical solutions. It necessitates an attitude that values innovation, creativity, and a readiness to question the existing quo.

## Fundamentals of Creative Design

# 1. User-Centricity

- **Objective:** Put an emphasis on resolving actual user issues.
- **Methods:**
  - Deep User Research
  - Empathy Mapping

**Outcome:** Solutions that are extremely relevant and beneficial to users.

# 2. Experimentation

- **Goal:** Promote taking chances and experimenting.

**Processes:**

- Fast prototyping
- A/B testing

**Result:** Creative solutions that arise from trial and error.

# 3. Collaboration

- **Goal:** Utilize a range of expertise and viewpoints.
- **Actions:**
  - Multifunctional Groups
  - Collaborative Art Workshops

**Result:** More complete answers and richer concepts.

# 4. Agility

- **Objective:** React promptly to developments and fresh perspectives.
- **Applications:**
  - Iterative Procedures
  - Agile Methodologies

**Result:** Flexible solutions that hold up throughout time.

# 5. Sustainability

- **Objective:** Consider long-term effects when designing.
- **Techniques:**
  - Eco-Friendly Materials
  - Ethical Design Practices

**Outcome:** Solutions that are environmentally and socially responsible.

## Methods of Promoting Innovation

# 1. Design Sprints

- **Objective:** Quickly test new ideas and find solutions to large issues.
- **Techniques:**

- ○ Time-Boxed Stages
- ○ Concentrated Group Work

**Result:** Innovative ideas are developed and validated quickly.

## 2. Blue Sky Thinking

- **Goal:** Promote unbridled creativity.
- **Activities:**
  - ○ Creative Idea Generation
  - ○ No Practicality Limitations
  - ○ Bold and creative ideas as the final product.

## 3. Trend Analysis

- **Goal:** Keep abreast of new developments in technology and patterns.
- **Methods:**
  - ○ Market Research
  - ○ Competitive Analysis

**Result:** Innovative solutions that take advantage of fresh opportunities

Developing innovative and design thinking skills is crucial to producing goods that not only address issues but also motivate and satisfy consumers. Through the implementation of an organized approach to design thinking, the utilization of various methods for ideation, the embracement of prototype and iteration, and the cultivation of an innovative culture, designers can create innovative solutions that are unique in the market and have a significant influence.

# CHAPTER 4

## Interaction Design and Information Architecture

## 4.1 Information Structure for Usability

The discipline of arranging and structuring content to improve findability and usability is known as information architecture, or IA. Creating a logical and unambiguous framework that facilitates efficient and easy information navigation is the aim.

### Important Information Architecture Components

### 1. Hierarchical Structure

- **Objective:** Logically and hierarchically arrange content.
- **Actions:**
  - Top-Down Approach: dividing large categories into smaller ones after they have been established.

     ○ Bottom-Up Approach: Classifying similar objects together into groups.

**Result:** A logical, well-organized framework that enables viewers to comprehend the connections between various content parts.

## 2. Labeling Systems

- **Objective:** Give content categories and navigation items succinct, understandable names.
- **Actions:**
  - ○ Consistency: Making certain that labels are the same all around the website.
  - ○ Clarity: Employing language that people are acquainted with and can understand.

**Result**: Labels that let readers navigate the information with ease.

## 3. Navigation Systems

- **Objective:** Provide user-friendly navigation that facilitates rapid information discovery.
- **Actions:**
  - ○ Global Navigation: Every page's primary navigation.

- Local Navigation: Content tailored to a certain area or webpage.

**Result:** A user-friendly navigation mechanism that makes content accessible quickly.

## 4. Search Systems

- **Objective:** Provide efficient search tools to assist users in locating particular information.
- **Actions:**
  - Position of the Search Bar: Making sure the search bar is accessible.
  - Advanced Search Options: Preserving and enhancing search results for users.

**Result:** A strong search engine that improves the findability of content.

## 5. Content Inventory and Audits

- **Objective:** Keep an exhaustive record of all content and conduct frequent checks to ensure accuracy and relevancy.
- **Actions:**
  - Content Inventory: A list of every item of content together with its location.

- material Audit: Assessing the relevance, correctness, and quality of material.

**Result:** A current and usable content library that is kept up to date and in good condition.

## 4.2 Creating Sense-Based Navigation

A positive user experience depends on intuitive navigation. It lessens frustration and raises user satisfaction by making it easy and quick for people to find what they're looking for.

## Fundamentals of Perceptual Navigation

## 1. Simplicity

- **Objective:** Maintain an easy-to-use and uncomplicated navigation system.
- **Actions:**
  - Minimalist Design: Steer clear of superfluous menu items and clutter.
  - Clear Labels: Make use of phrases that are easy to read and describe.

**Result:** User-friendly and easily understood navigation.

## 2. Consistency

- **Objective:** Make sure that the navigation components are the same on every page.
- **Actions:**
  - Standardized Layout: Maintaining the same placement for navigation menus.
  - Uniform Design: Employing standardized fonts, colors, and styles.

**Result:** A dependable and consistent navigation system for users.

## 3. Feedback

- **Objective:** Give consumers input regarding the navigation options they have selected.
- **Actions:**
  - Visual Cues: Emphasizing visited sites and active links.
  - Breadcrumbs: Displaying to users where they are in the site structure right now.

**Result:** Users are aware of where they are on the website and feel secure making navigational decisions.

# 4. Accessibility

- **Objective:** Guarantee that all users, including those with disabilities, can access the navigation.
- **Actions:**
    - Keyboard navigating: Utilizing keyboard shortcuts to enable navigating.
    - Screen Reader Compatibility: Guaranteeing that screen readers can read the navigation.

**Result:** An audience-diverse navigation system that is inclusive.


# 5. Mobile Responsiveness

- **Goal: Enhance mobile device navigation.**
- **Actions:**
    - Responsive design: modifying elements and layout to fit various screen sizes.
    - Touch-Friendly Elements: Making sure touchscreen navigation components are simple to tap.

**Result:** A smooth navigating experience on all platforms.

## 4.3 Principles of Interaction Design

The goal of interface design is to create productive and interesting user-digital product interactions. It entails creating components that make user actions easier and improve the user experience as a whole.

### Fundamental Ideas in Interaction Design

### 1. Affordability

- **Objective:** Utilize design features that imply their application.
- **Actions:**
  - Visual Cues: Signifying functioning with forms, colors, and textures.
  - Familiar Design Patterns: Making use of widely used, easily recognizable design patterns.

**Result:** Users interact with elements in an intuitive manner.

## 2. Feedback

- **Objective:** Respond to user actions right away with feedback.
- **Actions:**
  - Visual Feedback: Button highlights upon click or mouseover.
  - Auditory feedback: Signaling accomplishments or mistakes through sounds.

**Result:** Users are notified that their actions have been acknowledged and handled.

## 3. Consistency

- **Objective:** Ensure that interactions throughout the product are consistent.
- **Actions:**
  - Utilizing the same patterns for comparable actions is known as standard interaction patterns.
  - Uniform Visual Design: Making sure links, buttons, and other components have a consistent appearance and functionality.

**Result:** By being able to predict element behavior, users are less confused.

## 4. Efficiency

- **Objective**: Make jobs easy and quick for people to finish.
- **Actions:**
  - Simplified Workflows: Reducing the amount of steps needed to finish tasks.
  - Shortcuts: offering time-saving tools such as keyboard shortcuts.

**Result:** Users can accomplish their objectives with little difficulty.

## 5. Error Prevention and Recovery

- **Goal:** Reduce errors and offer solutions for overcoming them.
- **Actions:**
  - Preventive Measures: Forms and inputs are designed to avoid typical errors.
  - Clear problem Messages: Including remedies along with informative problem messages.

**Result:** Less mistakes are made by users, and when they do, they may bounce back fast.

## 4.4 Designing User Flows That Inspire

The routes users travel within a product to accomplish tasks are represented by user flows. A seamless and fulfilling user experience depends on designing user processes that are both entertaining and simple to use.

## How to Make Interesting User Flows

## 1. Define User Goals

- **Objective:** Recognize the objectives of users.
- **Actions:**
  - User research: Identifying user goals through surveys and interviews.
  - Task Analysis: Dividing tasks into their individual phases.

**Result:** A thorough comprehension of the goals of the user.

## 2. Develop User Journeys

- **Purpose:** Illustrate the actions users take to fulfill their objectives.
- **Actions:**
  - Flowcharts: Drawing user journeys as visual

aids.

- Storyboards: These show user interactions through visuals.

**Result:** An extensive user interaction map.

## 3. Design for Simplicity

- **Goal:** Make sure user flows are clear-cut and effective.
- **Actions:**
  - Minimal Steps: Cutting down on the amount of steps needed to finish a task.
  - Clear Navigation: Giving users alternatives and paths that are obvious.

**Result:** User flows that are simple to finish and follow.

## 4. Incorporate Feedback Loops

- **Goal:** Offer feedback to users at every stage of their journey.
- **Actions:**
  - Confirmation Messages: Informing users when their tasks have been accomplished successfully.
  - Progress Indicators: Showing steps or

progress bars.

**Result:** During their trip, users feel knowledgeable and assured.

## 5. Test and Iterate

- **Goal:** Constantly enhance user flows in response to input.
- **Actions:**
    - Usability testing involves seeing consumers interact with the flows.
    - A/B testing involves contrasting various iterations of user journeys.

**Result:** Improved user flows that improve the experience in general.

You can develop digital goods that are not just useful but also entertaining to use if you have a strong understanding of interface design and information architecture. A seamless and fulfilling user experience is mostly dependent on properly organizing information, developing interesting user flows, providing easy navigation, and abiding by interaction design principles.

# CHAPTER 5

## USER INTERFACE AND VISUAL DESIGN

## 5.1 Foundations of Visual Design

### Theory of Color

The foundation of visual design is color theory. It entails being aware of the interactions between colors, the feelings they arouse, and the useful combinations of colors.

**Primary, Secondary, and Tertiary Colors**:

1. **Primary:** Red, blue, and yellow are the primary colors; other colors cannot be combined to generate them.
2. **Secondary Colors:** made by combining basic colors, these include purple, orange, and green.
3. **Tertiary Colors:** Constructed from the combination of primary and secondary hues.

## Color Wheel

- It is a useful tool for comprehending complementary (opposite each other on the wheel), analogous (next to each other), and triadic (three colors evenly distributed around the wheel) color schemes.

- It is a visual depiction of colors grouped according to their chromatic connections.

## Color Harmony:

- The arrangement of colors in a visually pleasant way.

- Typical color schemes consist of complementary, triadic, analogous, and monochromatic variations in the luminance and saturation of a single hue.

## Psychology of Color

- states that various hues elicit distinct feelings and connotations.

- For instance, red can imply hurry and agitation, yet blue typically conjures up peace and confidence.

# Typography

The art and practice of arranging type to make written language understandable, legible, and aesthetically pleasing is known as typography.

## Fonts and Typefaces:

- **Serif Fonts:** such as Times New Roman have little lines or decorations at the ends of their letters.
- **Sans-Serif Fonts:** These fonts, like Arial, have fewer tiny lines and a cleaner appearance.
- **Script Fonts:** Often used for decoration, these fonts resemble cursive handwriting.

## Hierarchy and Readability:

- Using different font sizes, weights, and styles to create a visual hierarchy aids in directing the reader's attention.
- Font size, choice, line height, and letter spacing all affect readability.

## Spacing and Alignment:

- A neat and expert appearance is guaranteed by appropriate alignment (left, center, right, or justified).

- Good tracking, kerning, and leading—the distance between words and lines—all improve reading.

## Composition and Layout

The placement of visual components on a page or screen to create a harmonious and visually acceptable design is referred to as layout and composition.

## Grid Systems:

- Give layouts coherence and organization.
- Single-column, multi-column, and modular grid systems are common grid systems.

## White Space:

- The space that is left empty between pieces aids in attention-grabbing and clutter reduction. Often referred to as negative space, it enhances the design's overall readability and balance.

## Visual Hierarchy

- It refers to the placement, size, color, contrast, and

other design components arranged to convey significance.

## Alignment and Proximity:

- Verifies that the elements are arranged rationally and in alignment.
- Things that are near each other are viewed as connected.

## 5.2 Design Patterns for User Interfaces

## Design That Responds

A user interface (UI) that looks and works properly on a range of devices and screen sizes is guaranteed by responsive design.

## Fluid Grids:

- Instead of using fixed units like pixels, use relative units like percentages.
- Verify that the layout flows well across a range of screen sizes.

## Adaptive Images:

- Images can adjust in size and position within the layout without affecting the overall aesthetic.
- Attained by employing CSS properties such as {max-width: 100%;}.

## Media Queries:

- CSS method that applies styles according to the specs of the device, like screen size.
- Permits various layouts and designs for various devices.

## Design for Mobile

With a focus on touch interactions and small screens, mobile design optimizes user interfaces for smartphones and tablets.

## Touch Targets:

- Make sure interactive items and buttons are big enough to tap with ease.
- A minimum size of 44x44 pixels is advised.

## Simplified Navigation:

- Make use of clear menus and elements for easy access to the navigation.
- Use supplementary actions, such as swipes, to accomplish tasks.

## Content Prioritization:

- Give features and content that are the most important top priority.
- Use swipes or taps to reveal less crucial information by using progressive disclosure.

## Usability

By guaranteeing that a user interface (UI) can be used by individuals with impairments, accessibility improves inclusivity and complies with legal requirements.

## Keyboard Navigation:

- Verify that the keyboard can reach and operate all interactive items.
- Provide focus indications to indicate the selected element at any given time.

**Screen Reader Compatibility:**

- To enhance screen reader capability, make use of semantic HTML and ARIA (Accessible Rich Internet Applications) characteristics.
- Verify that screen readers can easily read and navigate all material.

**Color Contrast and Text Size:**

- Make sure the text and background have enough contrast.
- Make sure the text is readable at a comfortable size.

## 5.3 Developing Style Guides and Visual Language

**Pictorial Language**

All visual components utilized in a product are included in a visual language, which is a consistent design system that guarantees a unified appearance and feel.

**Color Palette:**

- A collection of colors that are used repeatedly in the

design; for versatility, include accent, secondary, and primary colors.

## Typography:

- A collection of typefaces and typographic designs applied to the entire product.
- Set line heights, font families, weights, and widths for various text elements.

## Iconography:

- A unified collection of icons that complement the general tone and design. Simple, instantly identifiable, and regularly utilized icons are ideal.

## Graphics and Images:

- Usage instructions for pictures, charts, and other visual components.
- Establish positioning, sizes, and styles to ensure uniformity.

## Style Manuals

A style guide is an extensive document that describes the

visual language and makes sure that all design and development work follows it.

## Components and Patterns:

- Detailed explanations of UI elements like forms, buttons, and navigation.
- Offer code snippets, usage directions, and examples.

## Design Principles:

- Fundamental ideas like simplicity, consistency, and clarity that direct design choices.
- Make sure these guidelines are followed in all designs.

## Brand Guidelines:

- Describe the brand's tone and visual elements.
- Incorporate brand voice, typography, color schemes, and logos.

You may provide a unified, captivating, and easily navigable user experience by being proficient in the principles of visual design, comprehending and applying user interface design patterns, and developing thorough visual language and style guides. These components are essential to making sure that your digital products look great and offer a smooth, engaging experience to all users.

# CHAPTER 6

## 6.1 Techniques for Usability Testing

A crucial step in user-centered design is usability testing, which entails assessing a product by putting it to the test on actual users. This aids in finding usability issues, gathering quantitative and qualitative information, and figuring out user happiness.

**Moderated Usability Testing:**

- Performed in the presence of a facilitator who will direct participants through tasks and pose follow-up queries.
- Offers in-depth understanding and permits prompt clarification and observation.

**Unmoderated Usability Testing:**

- Participants work alone to finish tasks, frequently

with the use of online technologies that log their conversations.

- Cost-effective and scalable, but not as deep as moderated sessions.

## Remote Usability Testing:

- A wide range of users can participate because participants are situated remotely.
- The ability to be either moderated or unmoderated offers ease and flexibility.

## In-Person Usability Testing:

- Performed under close observation in a controlled setting.
- Enables quick communication and feedback, but may require a lot of resources.

## Think-Aloud Protocol:

- As they work on tasks, participants express verbally their feelings, ideas, and behaviors.
- Identifies pain areas and offers insight into the mental processes of users.

## A/B Testing:

- Examines two iterations of a product to see which is more effective.

- Beneficial for deciding on design modifications based on data.

## Heuristic Evaluation:

- Professionals assess the product using accepted usability guidelines, or heuristics.

- Efficient and quick, yet could overlook problems unique to a user.

## 6.2 Collecting and Examining User Input

Gaining insight into the requirements, inclinations, and problems of users requires gathering and evaluating user input. Design choices and advancements are informed by this.

## Questionnaires and Surveys:

- Gather numerical information regarding user behavior, preferences, and satisfaction.

- Able to promptly contact a huge audience and offer

statistical insights.

## Interviews:

- Individual meetings to get detailed qualitative information.
- Permits investigation of user experiences, attitudes, and motives.

## Focus Groups:

- Group talks to elicit various viewpoints and identify recurring topics.
- Encourages discussion among users and can draw attention to areas of agreement and disagreement.

## User Feedback Tools:

- Support tickets, comment sections, and in-app feedback forms.
- Highlight recurring problems and offer real-time information.

## Reviewing Input:

- **Thematic Analysis:** Find trends and themes in the qualitative information.

- **Statistical Analysis:** For quantitative data, apply inferential and descriptive statistics.
- **Sentiment Analysis:** Use technologies for natural language processing to assess user sentiment.

## 6.3 Design Process Iterations

A product is continuously improved and refined through the iterative design process in response to user feedback and testing outcomes. This strategy guarantees that the product will adapt to suit user needs in an efficient manner.

**Design-Develop-Test Cycle:**
- **Design:** Produce mockups and prototypes in accordance with user input and preliminary specifications.
- **Develop:** Put the design into practice by creating working prototypes of the product.
- **Test:** To find problems and get input, run usability tests.

**Prototyping:**
- Create high-fidelity (interactive prototypes) and

low-fidelity (wireframes) models.

- Enables concept validation and early user testing.

## Continuous Feedback Loop:

- To improve and modify the product, incorporate user feedback into each cycle.
- Make sure that user ideas and identified usability concerns are incorporated into every iteration.

## Agile and Lean Methodologies:

- Iterate rapidly and effectively by utilizing lean concepts and agile sprints.
- Put your attention on making small, continuous improvements and growing with each iteration.

## 6.4 KPIs, or key performance indicators

KPIs are quantifiable figures that aid in assessing a product's efficacy and user experience. They shed light on how well the product satisfies customer demands and corporate objectives.

## Task Success Rate:

- Indicates the proportion of tasks that users finish successfully.
- A user-friendly design is indicated by high success rates.

## Time on Task:

- This feature keeps track of how long it takes users to finish a task.
- Quicker times indicate more effective and user-friendly interfaces.

## Error Rate:

- Indicates how many mistakes people make when doing a task.
- A more usable and error-tolerant design is shown by lower error rates.

## User Satisfaction:

- Measured via questionnaires and surveys, frequently with the use of metrics such as the Net Promoter Score (NPS) or System Usability Scale (SUS).
- Positive user experiences are indicated by high

satisfaction levels.

## Engagement Metrics:

- Incorporate data on page views, length of sessions, and frequency of interactions.
- A more engaging and practical product is usually correlated with more engagement.

## Conversion Rate:

- Indicates the proportion of visitors that finish a desired action (such as buying something or subscribing to a newsletter).
- Shows how well the product performs in reaching its intended business goals.

Through the implementation of diverse usability testing techniques, a methodical approach to obtaining and evaluating user input, iterative development grounded on that input, and vigilant observation of critical performance metrics, designers may guarantee that their products fulfill user requirements and yield outstanding user experiences. This procedure promotes user happiness and corporate success in addition to improving usability.

# CHAPTER 7

## NEW DEVELOPMENTS AND PROSPECTS

## 7.1 Artificial Intelligence's Place in UI/UX

By improving user experiences and expediting design procedures, artificial intelligence (AI) is transforming user interface/user experience (UI/UX) design.

**Personalization:**
- AI analyzes user data and behavior patterns to provide highly tailored user experiences.
- Tailored interactions produced by recommender systems, personalized information, and adaptable interfaces increase user engagement and happiness.

**Predictive Analytics:**
- Predictive analytics makes use of AI to foresee the requirements and actions of users.
- Enhances usability and user experience by assisting

designers in creating proactive and intuitive interfaces.

## Automated Design Tools:

- Artificial intelligence (AI)-driven design tools help designers by automating tedious activities and making design suggestions.
- The design process is streamlined by programs like Adobe Sensei and Sketch's Smart Layout, freeing up designers to concentrate on creativity and problem-solving.

## Natural Language Processing (NLP):

- NLP improves user interfaces by enabling chatbots and conversational agents.
- Enhances user interactions by responding quickly, accurately, and contextually.

## User Behavior Analysis:

- Artificial intelligence examines user interactions to pinpoint problems and potential areas for development.
- Data-driven design choices are influenced by

heatmaps, session recordings, and user path analysis.

## 7.2 Voice Interface Design

Voice interfaces are becoming more and more common, providing accessible, effective, and hands-free means of interacting with technology.

**Voice User Interface (VUI) Design Principles:**
- Give conversational design and natural language interactions priority.
- Make sure that voice prompts and responses are concise, clear, and easy to understand.

**Context Awareness:**
- Create speech interfaces that are sensitive to and cognizant of the context of their users.
- Contextual awareness enhances user experience by increasing accuracy and relevance.

**Multimodal Interactions:**
- For a more engaging user experience, pair voice interfaces with tactile or visual components.

- Multimodal interactions take into account the various demands and preferences of users.

## Error Handling:

- To control misunderstandings and user annoyance, use strong error handling.
- Offer succinct, precise feedback and recommend remedial measures.

## Accessibility:

- Voice interfaces are incredibly beneficial for users with disabilities in terms of accessibility.
- Make sure the design is inclusive and compatible with assistive devices.

## 7.3 Virtual and Augmented Reality Experiences

Due to their ability to create immersive and engaging experiences, augmented reality (AR) and virtual reality (VR) are revolutionizing UI/UX design.

## AR in UI/UX:

- AR improves in-person interactions by

superimposing digital data on the real environment.

- Applications that provide compelling and context-aware experiences include shopping, education, and navigation.

## VR in UI/UX:

- VR produces completely immersive settings that let people engage with virtual spaces.
- Rich, dynamic, and realistic experiences are provided through the use of virtual tours, gaming, and training.

## AR/VR Design Considerations:

- Put user comfort and ergonomics first to reduce pain and motion sickness.
- Guarantee easy navigation and engagement in three-dimensional environments.

## User-Centered Design in AR/VR:

- Use feedback and iterative testing to include users in the design process.
- Address AR/VR-specific usability issues including gesture recognition and spatial awareness.

Technological Integration:

- For improved functionality, combine AR/VR with other technologies like AI and IoT.
- A seamless integration guarantees an integrated and all-encompassing user experience.

## 7.4 UI/UX Design: Ethical Considerations

In order to ensure that technology maximizes advantages while reducing harm, ethical issues are crucial in UI/UX design.

**Privacy and Data Security:**

- Give user privacy and data security a priority when making design choices.
- Establish secure data storage and transparent data procedures to foster user confidence.

**Inclusive Design:**

- Take into account the demands of all users while designing with diversity and inclusivity in mind.
- Steer clear of prejudices and preconceptions when

designing to guarantee fair access and experiences.

## Sustainable Design:

- Take into account how design decisions may affect the environment.
- Select eco-friendly products and methods to reduce your environmental impact.

## User Well-Being:

- Create user interfaces that support psychological and mental wellness.
- Steer clear of manipulative design techniques (such dark patterns) that take advantage of user psychology.

## Ethical AI and Automation:

- Make sure AI and automation are applied in an ethical manner, free from bias and discrimination.
- Uphold accountability and openness in interactions powered by AI.

Designers may produce unique, moral, and user-focused experiences by keeping up with current trends and new fields. UI/UX design will continue to develop and fulfill user wants and expectations in a constantly evolving technological context by embracing AI, voice interfaces, AR/VR, and ethical issues.

## ABOUT THE AUTHOR

Author and thought leader in the IT field Taylor Royce is well known. He has a two-decade career and is an expert at tech trend analysis and forecasting, which enables a wide audience to understand complicated concepts.

Royce's considerable involvement in the IT industry stemmed from his passion with technology, which he developed during his computer science studies. He has extensive knowledge of the industry because of his experience in both software development and strategic consulting.

Known for his research and lucidity, he has written multiple best-selling books and contributed to esteemed tech periodicals. Translations of Royce's books throughout the world demonstrate his impact.

Royce is a well-known authority on emerging technologies

and their effects on society, frequently requested as a speaker at international conferences and as a guest on tech podcasts. He promotes the development of ethical technology, emphasizing problems like data privacy and the digital divide.

In addition, with a focus on sustainable industry growth, Royce mentors upcoming tech experts and supports IT education projects. Taylor Royce is well known for his ability to combine analytical thinking with technical know-how. He sees a time when technology will ethically benefit humanity.

www.ingramcontent.com/pod-product-compliance
Lightning Source LLC
LaVergne TN
LVHW051539050326
832903LV00033B/4325